WANDLORE
A GUIDE FOR THE APPRENTICE WANDMAKER

WANDLORE

A GUIDE FOR THE APPRENTICE WANDMAKER

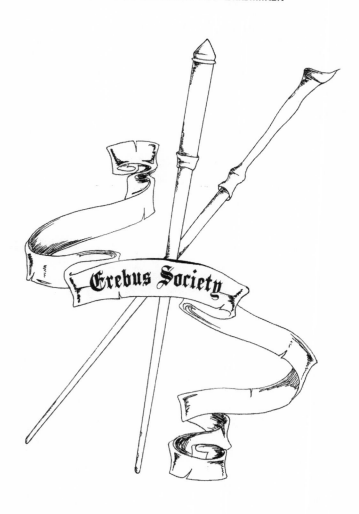

Erebus Society

K. P. THEODORE

Erebus Society
Glasgow

First published in Great Britain in 2015
Erebus Society
Glasgow

Revised Edition

ISBN 978-0-9933284-0-4

CONTENTS

WANDLORE

Wandlore is a very ancient branch of magick that dates back to thousands of years ago in ancient civilisations like the Ancient Greeks, the Sumerians, the Babylonians, the Celts etc. Wandlore focuses on the study of wands, their history, their attributes, materials, abilities, actions, characteristics and the way of crafting them.

One of the most famous wand-holders was Hermes (Greek: Ἑρμῆς) also known as Mercury from the Romans. Before he became an Olympian God, or better to say, earn the title of it, Hermes was a physical person, a historical figure. Hermes according to the historians was born in Kyllini of Arcadia (Greek: Κυλλήνη της Αρκαδίας) in Greece around 9.000 B.C., the era that the ancient Greeks named "Era of the Gods". He was the son of Mea (Μαία), daughter of the King of Peloponnisos Atlantas ('Ατλαντας). His wife was Ersi ('Ερση) daughter of the king of Athens Kerkopas (Κέρκοπας).

In his time, among all the things he did and the teachings he offered, Hermes was very well known for his 7 principles, the principles that according to him ruled the world. These principles are:

First Principle
"Speech is everything. The Universe is a state of Mentality"

Meaning that everything we see and observe around us, only exists because intellect exists.
Nothing exists without someone to observe or create it and everything can manifest and exist if some one has the will it requires to become real. Mind over matter and reality.

Second Principle
"Whatever is above, so it is bellow. Whatever is bellow, so it is above"

This is the root of the well known these days As above so Bellow. The second principle is about the form of the universe, that Earth and Heavens have the same form, the same principles of existence.

Third Principle
"Nothing is motionless, everything vibrates"

This is also known by another Greek philosopher, Heraclitus of Ephesus (Greek: Ἡράκλειτος ὁ Ἐφέσιος) c. 535 – c. 475 BCE who said "Everything Flows" (Τα πάντα ρεῖ – Ta *panta rhei*). According to both of them, everything in existence moves, everything has a flow and a vibration. The Universe itself might not move but everything inside it, all of it's materials visible or not, they move. From the water in the earth, the blood inside us, to the soil of the planet and the explosions inside a star, nothing remains stable and still, everything moves, shifts and changes all the time.

Fourth Principle
"Everything is dual, everything is bipolar. Everything is a pair of opposites, the ends meet."

A reference to the magnetic poles of the earth, the planets and the stars, and also of the magnetic elements of the nature, even the particles within every existing thing. The ends that meet is the pairing of opposites, the natural attraction of the heteronymous among the elements of nature, the opposite charged particles, the personalities, the states of existence and everything dual.

Fifth Principle
"Everything flows and flows again. Everything has periods of prosperity and decline, ascent and descent. Everything moves like a pendulum. The measure of the movement to the right is the same with the measure of the movement to the left. The rhythm is their equation."

It is the observable movement from the flow of everything in the universe. The reference of the pendulum is nothing more than the equal changes between matter or energy in different physical or not phenomena that they can be explained with today's science, for example the Newton's law of Motion, the Momentum and Impulse Connection, the Momentum and Law of Conservation of Energy and more. The measure and rhythm are about the stable movement and equality of the pendulum.

Sixth Principle
"Every cause has it's result. Every result has a cause, everything happens according to the Law"

This is the origin of the Law of Action – Reaction and the universal principle of this observable phenomenon. Can apply to both physical and non physical events.

Seventh Principle
"Birth exists everywhere. Everything has a male and a female origin. Birth manifests on every level."

A reference to the reproduction of life, the conjugation of male and female. From the most usual of examples to the single cell organisms and the birth of stars and worlds (manifests on every level).

These are the basic principles of existence on short analysis according to Hermes, and are principles that find place in Wandlore as well as the flow of energy and the laws of universe apply on everything within it, the every day life, the laws of Magick, the wands etc.

✳

Hermes had also a son with his wife. His name was Tat (Τατ). After his life, Hermes gained the title of Olympian God, which is the more or less he equivalent with today's saints, although the Olympian God Title has the position of a deity in the hierarchy. When he died, his son Tat travelled to Egypt and started teaching his father's word, sharing the philosophical knowledge with the people of the area, mentoring and educating anyone he could, from common people to royals. This gave him the title of the ancient Egyptian God Thoth, who is the god of letters and knowledge.

✳

The first well famed wand we know of belonged to Hermes. Kerykeion (Greek: κηρύκειον *kērukeion* which translates to herald's staff) or Caduceus in Latin (page 5), was a short staff/wand which consisted of twin serpents/snakes wrapped around it from bottom to top, and had twin wings mounted at it's top just before the wand's tip. The handle and the shaft of the wand were made of wood and the serpents and wings were made of bronze. Unfortunately we do not have any proven information about the type of the wood used. We can only do speculations about it based on it's master's nature but it will remain an inaccurate information.

4

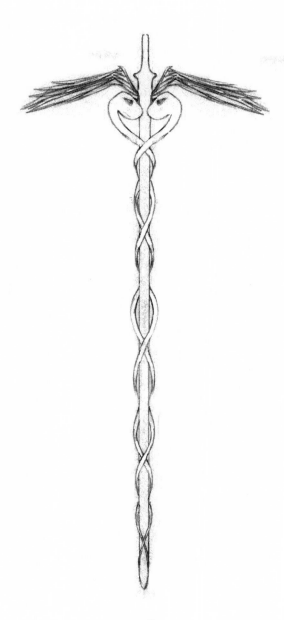

Some times, especially in the modern days, people misuse the symbolism of Kerykeion and confuse it with the staff of Asclepius which is a symbol of health and medicine (page 7). The obvious difference though except all symbolism, use and qualities, is that the staff of Asclepius also known as the Rod of Asclepius is a long staff with a single snake wrapped around it and no wings mounted on the top of it.

This branch of magick is too complex to master and thus there are very few really skilled and capable Wandmakers around the world. To become one and study the lore, one must become an apprentice of a skilled wandmaker, this includes having an advanced level of occult and magical studies of course. It is a long and hard process and requires a natural gift, patience and determination.

WANDS

Wands are magickal tools used by practitioners to manipulate and focus energy, cast spells, banish sigils, create concoctions, do ritual working and more. The term practitioner in this book is an umbrella to include other terms such as witch, sorcerer and any other ones involved in the practices of the occult and magick. Some call wands "psychic pens" as they can also be used to "draw" symbols, sigils, shapes and inscriptions on objects, locations and mid air to be used for various personal workings.

A wand, like other tools in magickal practice, is considered a somehow sentient tool. That's because strong bonds are formed between a wand and it's owner. These are mental, spiritual, emotional and magickal bonds that make a wand appear as if it has it's own intelligence when interacting with it's owner. Also the wood and especially the core of the wand, give it that special touch that we could call it it's "personality".

All the above make each wand to be unique and give it its special treats and characteristics that make it react in various ways while in different situations or kinds of magick.

They can be made of various woods, have different cores and essences, be decorated with miscellaneous materials and have a variety of lengths, widths and shapes. All these aspects add to the special characteristics of each wand and make it like no other.

Although all that looks neat and easy to understand, some of even the most skilled and experienced wandmakers fail to fully comprehend how wands really work. They know what to do and how to combine every single thing in a right way to make each desired wand, but they might not truly know how and why these things work all together.

As a wandmaker once told me: "I know how to make them and I have knowledge of all their materials. I know they work but I do not understand why or how!"

Of course we know "how" wands work in spellcasting. When they say they don't know why or how they mean that other than its function they do not comprehend how these things combined all together create something like that and make it work.

The wands as complete magickal tools function in a very complex way that need a whole book to explain and a completely different approach. For a very quick explanation we can say that wands other than conductors or amplifiers of bio/magickal energy, mostly work as triggers to cause instant changes to the state of the practitioner's mind in order to cast a spell.

First of all, the use of such a unique tool that cannot really be used for any other reason create a sense of a magickal state instantly to the practitioner's mind especially when someone gets used to it in time. The moves made during a casting or an energy manipulation are very specific and they are "engineered" in such a way that they can alter the brain function, shift mentality and trigger different states in the user's mind. The shape, the texture, the smell, add to it and create an even more personalised bond with the magickal state and the wand itself. Finally each spell, before it is ready to be cast has to be prepared with a series of techniques, each with a different approach.

Mastering the skill of visualisation is the key, in a level that the practitioner is able to create optical illusions in the physical plane of existence. A spell is been prepared for example through meditation, visualisation and various other techniques, someone can say like a small ritual so it can be registered in the practitioner's inner mind. When something gets registered that way it always exists and can never been really forgotten.

Then all the process gets banished from the conscious mind the same way that someone banishes sigils in order for them to work in the future.

When all that is done in a very profound way of course (this is just a rough explanation not instructions) the spell awaits to be used. Then the wand movements and the spell's incantation which might be just a single word, create correlation links that can instantly trigger the practitioner's subconscious and recreate the exact same state as when the spell was getting registered, thus each spell can therefore be recreated instantly in an almost automatic way as long as the one who is going to cast it has studied it deeply and done the proper procedures in the past.

FUNDAMENTAL PRINCIPLES OF WANDS

The wand itself is influencing its future owner to choose it and not the other way round. Even when one chooses their own wand out of a selection of ready made wands, its the wand's shape, colour, and feeling that influences towards the selection. When one is crafting their wand then the certain qualities of the future wand is what influences the wand maker to go for this options and make the choice.

The only situation that the choice of the wand falls entirely to the practitioner is when they want a wand of specific attributes and qualities for very specialised workings.

Working with a wand is a complex process with mysterious connections between the wand and the owner, that takes time, effort and patience to be achieved.

There are various activation and enchanting rituals for the wands, each wandmaker has their own personalised one. There is not such thing though as a bonding ritual or a spell to bind a wand to its owner. Bonding with a wand is solely based upon the owner-wand cooperation and can only be achieved with effort, determination, constant working and time.

Through the cooperation between the wand and the owner, the one learns from the other. The wand as a "sentient" tool learns from its owner and adapts to their way of spellcasting and style of magick, and the owner learns from the wand and adapts to it's own little "personality". This learning journey is what makes some wands to work better for some owners than others. It is a relation of adoption and adaptation.

Every practitioner/caster can channel their bio/magickal energy almost through any wand that can belong to anyone. The best results though come only where the practitioner and the wand are connected or liked by each other, usually by a long-term partnership. Same as with most other tools used in the occult arts and crafts.

When a wand is severely damaged or snapped it cannot be repaired, thus is no longer usable.

CRAFTING THE WAND

CRAFTING THE WAND

For someone to become a wandmaker, wood-crafting skills are useful but not nearly enough. A wand maker must first understand all aspects of magick, spellcasting, all possible uses of magick wands, their nature, their characteristics and also have a wide experience with the observation of different magick and casting styles in order to be able to think of, design and create each wand on the highest standards.

Wood-crafting skills of course are essential for each wandmaker, but it is something that can be taught along the way of someone's apprenticeship. The only few mandatory things for someone to even start considering to become a wand maker is a magickal talent, willing to learn, a very open neutral mind and a great love for wands and the arts of the occult.

The universal principles that Hermes first mentioned, are very useful for one to understand the flow of energy, the use of wands and other occult tools, to comprehend things about the environment we live and act and eventually become a master in wandlore able to deliver top notch wands that will cast spells with optimal results.

Things to be considered before and during wand crafting.
The wood
The core
The length
The shape
Decorations

THE WOOD

The wood used, has to be of a high quality wood suitable for wandmaking. This type of wood except of being of a great physical quality and condition, has to be classified as either magickal or taken from an enchanted tree or to be natural and strong enough to sustain the magick power that will be embedded in it during the enchantments.

Magickal and Enchanted trees refer to an old wandmakers' tradition in which every wand maker plants their own trees and place enchantments over them. These trees are then used solely for the purpose of wandmaking. On the other hand wand-grade wood can be found in any tree and does not need to come from an enchanted one. It has always to be natural without being processed, as it happens for example in most of the wood that comes from a timber mill. Best option is the branches of living trees.

The wood itself as a variety can be from many tree species and each give special characteristics to the wand. Choosing the correct wood for each wand is highly important for an effective wand that will deliver top notch performances. Each wood has it's own attributes and properties. Different woods re used to create different types of wand for different paths of magick or styles of spellcasting. Some can be used for very specific types of magick while some others are very versatile and can be used for a great range of spells and paths.

Wands made from a combination of two different woods is essential to have a long core from edge to edge so the energy can flow through it without getting interrupted in the joints and also to be transferred from one type of wood to the other.

It is not recommended though to have wands made of more than a single type of wood or even of more than a single piece of wood. It works in a much more efficient way to have a homogenized structure though the entire wand.

TYPES OF WOOD

Alder (Alnus Rubra)

The Wanderer, The one who crosses between worlds, The Seer.

This wood is best used to create bridges between worlds and connections between life and death. It is an excellent wood to use for oracular magick, bridging, concealment and any kind of divination.

Wands made of of Alder seek the companion of someone who is a traveler in both the physical and the spiritual plane, someone who sees what others cannot see and communicates with the beyond. These wands are also ideal for preservation spells and resurrection rituals as they are highly connected with immortality.

Origination: West coast of North America

Alder

Applewood (Malus Domestica)

The pure of heart, The peace maker, The Healer.

This is one of the best woods to be used for healing magick and rituals or practices of nourishment. It works really well for the innocuous kinds of divination magick. Applewood wands produce the most positive of vibes thus won't work well for offensive spells and harmful magick, most of the times they might even "refuse" to produce such spells, with the exception of emergency situation in which their owner must use every spell in their "arsenal".

As their nature suggests, these wands go better with a companion of a pure heart, someone uninterested in dark magick, someone who wants to make the world a better place and has visions of becoming a pacifier or healer.

Origination: West Asia and Europe

Ash (Fraxinus Americana)

The Strong and Determined, The Protector.

Ash is the wood of duality and the marriage of opposites. One of the best woods to be used for protection and healing magick. It can also be used for rituals that deal with traveling between worlds and between life and death. This sturdy wood provides the wandmakers what they need to make a strong bold wand for someone with the spirit of the hero within. Wands made of this wood need an aspiring owner with strong will. They are also some of the most capable wands when it comes to weather magick.

Some suggest that an ash wand's master will likely be a person with a good, great but also stubborn personality and for that reason ash wands cannot be gifted from one owner to another or passed from one generation to the next because they tend to adapt to the stubbornness of their previous owner and "refuse" to work for anyone else.

Orientation: the east of the United States

Aspen (Populus Tremuloides)

The Shifter, The Duelist, The Revolutionary.

Aspen wood is best for those with a dual personality. Owners of wands made of aspen tend to be these people with the pure kind face and an underlying ability to destroy. The ones who want to do good but can also be harmful to others if the circumstances demand. Those who look very gentle and might tremble in the presence of fear, but when challenged they can be strong and aggressive.

Aspen wands, as their ideal owner's personality suggest, can be used for either good or bad magick. They are great for protection and healing as well as for hexing and cursing. The right practitioner matched correctly with an aspen wand will excel in the field of charmwork and combat magick.

Origination: The north part of the United States and Canada

Australian Blackwood (Acacia Melanoxylon)

The neutral state, The Inbetween.

This is a wood to be used for the wand of someone who is neutral and takes no sides. For someone indifferent to good or evil, to light or darkness. Wands made of Australian Blackwood can be used for both creating and destroying, for healing and hexing, for repelling and also casting curses. They are very versatile and will work well for almost anyone.

They will reveal their true potential though only when used by someone who is truly neutral and will use the wand for both light and dark, for multiple purposes. These wands have to be used by someone who has strength and determination within.

Origination: Australia

Australian Blackwood

Avodire (Turraeanthus Africanus)

Creativity and Imagination.

This wood is excellent for defensive and protective magick. Avodire wands are best given as first practice wands to young practitioners who will follow the "white" path, as they are best used for positive non harmful magick and they require the companion of someone with a vivid imagination and a lot of creativity. Imaginative and creative practitioners that happen to be the owners of a wand made of avodire, will thrive in all sorts of creative magic, new beginnings and even mundane every day projects that bring something new to our lives.

Avodire wands can also be used by those adults who possess a childish heart that mean no harm.

Origination: Cameroon, Ivory Coast and Nigeria

Beech (Fagus)

The Tolerant, The open minded, The one who is wiser than their age.

A wand made of beech is a great wand to be used by those who seek knowledge and true wisdom. It is brilliant for spiritual work and practices that create illumination of the mind. Beech wands are also excellent for producing fine charms and enchantments.

Wands made of beech wood will only work to their true potential when they find their perfect match as an owner and companion. This will be someone understanding, who is seeking to learn and live their life in a truthful way. For the one who has an open mind and is willing to explore new ideas, new areas, new places and practices, and who does not discriminate others based on taboos and prejudice.

Origination: Asia, Europe and North America

Birch (Betula Papyrifera)

The pure of heart, The Protector.

This is one of the best woods to be used for purification and protection. Excellent for defensive and protection spells, cleansing, shielding, warding, purification rituals and all sorts of supportive magick.

Birch wands will seek the companion of the one who intends to use non harmful magick, the one who is a friend of nature and they will thrive in the hands of someone who has the chances and potential of becoming a great protector and healer.

Origination: Europe and North America

Black Laurel (Laurus Nobilis)

The fighter against the dark forces.

In contradiction with its name, black laurel is a wood which is excellent at destroying the energies of dark magick. A wand made of black laurel will be the perfect tool to counter dark magick and reverse negative spells, jinxes, hexes and curses.

Black laurel wands match well with those individuals who dream of a world without evil, who protest for the people's rights and are always first in line to fight against the dark forces in an either mundane or magickal way.

Origination: Morocco and Spain

Black Laurel

Black Limba (Terminalia Superba)

The Indifferent and Neutral.

This is a powerful wood to work with when it comes to dark magick, for both protection from it or using and casting it. It is a very dual wood that makes wands able to make an excellent defense against dark magick tool that can cast the most powerful of protective spells, but also produce powerful hexes and curses.

Wands made of black limba are completely neutral and will work well for almost any kind of companion. The good the bad or the neutral. Although, one might find difficult to use a wand made of this wood to only practice in a certain way or path. By their nature they seek variety and thus their best match as an owner will be someone completely indifferent in terms such as greater good or personal gain.

Origination: Africa

Black Poisonwood (Metopium Brownei)

The Strong and Neutral.

This wood is the Mexican equivalent to the black limba. Neutral and strong wands made of this wood are excellent for both defending from and producing dark magick.

Black poisonwood wands are indifferent to a path or purpose and can be used by almost any kind of practitioner, regardless of their intentions. These wands excel in the hands of those who possess a strong will and are loyal in their cause, they mostly seek a powerful and determined companion.

Origination: Mexico

Blackthorn (Prunus Spinosa)

The Warrior, The loyal one.

One of the darkest in character woods, blackthorn is one of the strongest and excellent woods for dark magick. It is extremely hard and calls for a strong personality. Wands made of blackthorn wood, will seek the companion of a true warrior in spirit, someone confident who is not doubting their abilities. A blackthorn wand can produce great defensive spells as well, but due to its nature of being able to produce destructive energies, in that case, offensive spells are the best defense.

One can only be truly bonded with a blackthorn wand when they pass through danger and difficult times together, and then it can become a loyal friend and servant for life.

Origination: United Kingdom and Northern Ireland

Black Walnut (Juglans Nigra)

Honesty and Insight.

A very strong wood in both physical and magickal meaning that is excellent for any kind of charms and positive magick. Wands made of black walnut "behave" in a different way than most wands. They will only work well with someone who is truthful and honest, with someone who is self aware, who refuses to deceive themselves or others.

If the above characteristics are met, black walnut wands will work well for most spells and charms and even though they are identified as "white-positive" wands, they can work with dark magick if the circumstances require. They will work for almost anything as long as their owner is truthful to their cause and really want to do so.

Origination: The Eastern part of North America

Bloodwood
(Haematoxylum Campechianum)

The Strong and Passionate.

This is a great wood to work with for almost and kind of magick and especially healing. Bloodwood wands will be guided by their master's emotional state and their levels of emotional completeness. They are wands capable of producing the most complex kinds of spells, but they will only do their best during a certain emotional state or discharge caused by love, fear or anger.

They are extremely versatile and they are indifferent in paths, sides and ways of practice. As long as emotions are important to their owner, bloodwood wands will work wonders. It doesn't matter if the emotion is negative or positive, if it is driven by ambition, lust, desire, greed etc. for that is the important "fuel" to keep its magick going. Some times though these wands might seem to "wither" and not working properly, when their owner falls in states of emotional imbalance or simply the emotional states are that low that will create a feeling of internal emptiness.

Origination: Mexico

Bocote (Cordia Alliodora)

Intelligence and Creativity.

This wood is best used for mental work, practices that induce inspiration and techniques that strengthen the mind. Bocote wands will seek for a companion someone of high intelligence and those who possess a lot of imagination. It is almost the equivalent of avodire, in a way that can be used a lot by adults and is not limited to adults with a childish heart or those who have it since their child or teenage years. A difference between these two though is that bocote is much more versatile than avodire.

Bocote it is an indifferent, neutral wood so it will work well for both white and dark magick. Wands made of bocote are excellent for spells that deal with persuasion, concentration and mental abilities, although they can be used for almost any kind of magick.

Origination: America

Buckeye (Aesculus Glabra)

The Healer.

Buckeye is one of the best woods that have been used for healing. Wands made of this wood will seek a true healer to be their companion as they are excellent for healing spells, medical magick and curse banishing.

The fact that buckeye wands are some of the best tools for healing, should not confuse anyone that one with such a wand is of pure intentions. Healing is not a privilege of those who practice non harmful magick or those of pure intentions. Healing is something that everyone needs at some point no matter what's their path or way of practice. A healer can work for either good or evil and can heal something from a "disease" but can also heal a disease from its cure.

Origination: United States

Canary Wood (Centrolobium Ochryxylon)

The Achiever.

A very versatile wood that can be used for any kind of magick. Canary wood wands work best with the companion of someone who is determined to achieve their goals no matter what it takes to do so and regardless the consequences. These wands are indifferent between good or evil, they can be used for most magickal workings, for a variety of spells, paths and practices. They are best used for techniques that involve control and want to achieve manipulation and they are also excellent wands for charmwork.

It is common to find this wood in wands and magickal tools amongst those who achieved authority and high social status through their constant will and determination to achieve at all costs and those who used manipulation techniques to do so, such as priests, politicians, ministers etc.

If a canary wood wand is matched with the proper companion, it will cooperate beautifully and encourage its master.

Origination: Brazil

Cedar (Juniperus Virginiana)

The Protector, The Loyal one, The Strong within.

Even though cedar wood is good for most magickal practices, in almost all cases it will match with a "white" companion with a very strong character, someone who is loyal to their cause and want to protect others and especially their loved ones. Cedar wands are great for most spells but they excel in the protective ones. They are excellent for warding off, repulsing and block negative energies and dark magick.

It is best used for non harmful practices unless it is a great need, even though it can be perfectly matched some times with the practitioners of a dark path. In that case they will still follow their path, but it is those practitioners who are not doing direct damage, those who are finding indirect, stealthy ways to cause harm.

Origination: North America

Cedar

Cherry (Prunus Serotina, Prunus Serrulata)

Harmony, Strangeness.

Cherry wood is excellent for divination and healing magick. Since it is a wood of harmony, wands made of cherry will seek someone with exceptional willpower and self control, otherwise they can be turned to massive troublemakers with severe consequences even for their own master's.

Cherry wood wands are exceptional for divination techniques and healing magick as mentioned before, they are also fantastic at casting binding spells. A very skilled practitioner matched with a cherry wand can cast the most powerful of binding charms that seem almost unbreakable to others.

Origination: North America, Europe, Asia (Japan)

Chestnut (Castanea Spp.)

The Nourishing, The Protective, The one Guided by Love.

This is a wood that seeks those who are willing to succeed and are guided by their motivations and love to achieve their life's goals, no matter what their nature. Wands made of chestnut will work well for any kind of companion, because all natures, even the darkest ones have love for something and want to succeed of course. Also because chestnut wands' "personality" is only completed by their companions, what is missing will fill in from their master's nature and character, and will adapt to it.

There is another observation that suggests that chestnut wands are great for herbalists and those who practice natural ways of magick.

They are good for most kinds of spells and excellent for protection, healing and they promote creativity.

Origination: The Northern Hemisphere of America and Europe

Cocobolo (Dalbergia Retusa)

The Night Owl, The one who Empowers others.

Cocobolo is a wood that can provide wands which are very specialised in nocturnal and lunar magick. Only the heart of the wood can give proper wood of wand-grade quality and standards so a wandmaker can craft a fully functional wand.

Wands made of cocobolo are good for absolutely any kind of spell. They are also great at increasing the power of rituals and raising energy especially when a lunar based technique is used or when the practitioner works during the night. These wands are also known for magnifying a lot their master's own magickal "skills" at most times of the day and especially in the winter. The winter solstice, the new and the full moon are the days that a practitioner can reach the peak of a cocobolo wand's abilities.

Origination: Central America

Cypress (Cupressus sp.)

Nobility, The Spirit-whisperer, The Hero.

The cypress wood makes very powerful wands for the determined practitioners. A wand made of this wood is a neutral wand thus can be used by practitioners of any path without discriminating. Although cypress wands can go with anyone, they will truly match only with those of a heroic heart, no matter their goal, with those who have bravery and self-sacrifice as their most important qualities.

Wands made of cypress are exceptional for all types of spells and paths and can be used in a variety of practices. They excel at spells that can help their owner stick to their path, such as healing, protecting, empowering even hexing, cursing and obliterating. They are the perfect example to support the old saying that "A magickal tool is only as good and strong as its owner is".

Origination: The Northern Hemisphere of Africa, America and Asia

Cypress

Dogwood (Cornus Kousa)

The Playful personality.

Dogwood is a versatile wood and can work for both white and dark magick. It has a very neutral and playful nature and wands made of this wood will mostly seek a companion of someone who can be both playful and serious, quirky and mature at the same time when circumstances demand.

They work great for most spells but they show their true abilities when their owner is under pressure. They are excellent, someone can say some of the best, when it comes to charmwork and all sorts of enchantments.

Origination: Eastern Asia

Ebony (Diospyros Crassiflora)

The Non-Conformist, The Diverse, The Strong, The Dominant.

Ebony is considered to be the most powerful of woods when it comes to the the art of wandmaking, and it is a wood that will deliver pure, strong and almost ultimate power. This will be the hundred percent of what its master has inside. Wands made of ebony are indifferent of their master's path and they will perform protective, healing, dispelling, in other words white path spells, as well as offensive, destructive spells and magick from the darkest of arts.

Ebony wands are very versatile and they seek someone versatile as well, with a strong personality, someone who will have the courage to be themselves, and are prepared to face anything and anyone without fear for the consequences.

It makes an excellent wand for those who draw power from the darkest parts of the soul, the inner self, those who hide secrets and who are in touch with the spirit realm. Perfect for enchantments and blasts of aggressive raw power. They are considered to be some of the best tools for non-verbal magick, because of their connection with their master's subconscious and conscious mind.

Origination: East and South Africa

Ebony

Elder (Sambucus spp.)

The Healer, The Protector, The Fae Traveler.

Elder wood is associated with white magick and the faerie realm. Wands made of elder should be used for healing, protection, death rituals and funerals, and non harmful magick. These wands are ideal for those who like to help others and are in contact with forests, faery entities and nature's spirits.

Wands made of elder are excellent protection tools and companions but they are very tricky to be truly mastered. It takes time, long time, and a very pure heart for someone to be the perfect companion of an elder wand. For those who seek union with nature, peace and true wisdom, elder wands are a brilliant choice.

Origination: Eastern North America, Europe

Elm (Ulmus Glabra)

The Neutral, The Elegant, The Sophisticated.

This is a completely neutral wood that can be used for both protecting and attacking, healing from harm and causing it as well. Elm wands are excellent for dark magick that can be used for both defense or offense, as they draw their power from the darkness. Wands made of elm will seek a strong companion, someone sophisticated, very sophisticated actually, capable of casting very advanced spells and enchantments in the most elegant way.

They are great for opening gates to the realm of shadows, for hexing, protecting and for producing destructive spells. Even though an elm wand comes from a dark nature, it can be used for the most noble of causes as well. Darkness isn't only bad and destruction is not either. Someone can use these qualities to throw darkness to those who cause harm and destroy the obstacles that stand in the way of a good cause.

Origination: Greece and the United Kingdom

Eucalyptus (Eucalyptus Regans)

The Protection, The Nourishing, The Healer.

Eucalyptus is a great wood for healing and protection. It is not that commonly used though, probably because of its origination that made it unpopular in Europe even when we had the means to access its supplies.

Wands made of eucalyptus are excellent for handling lunar energies, casting some of the most powerful of healing spells and produce strong protective enchantments even over large areas. Their best companion are those who enjoy taking care of others and find pleasure in making those around them overcome their problems and feel well. These wands are also somehow versatile and depending on the case or current need they can be used for most kinds of spells and magickal techniques.

Origination: Australia

Eucalyptus

Fig (Ficus Carica)

The Healer.

Fig is a very uncommon wood for wand making. It is so because it can only be properly used for healing purposes. It becomes popular though when it comes to the circles of healing practitioners and shamanism. For the obvious reasons. Wands made of fig are brilliant for energy raising and manipulation for healing spells, enchantments and rituals and make some of the best healing tools for the witch nurses.

Other types of spells will probably fail to be cast successfully most of the times no matter who the wand's owner is. For someone who wants to go with a fig wand for life and not just to use it as a healing tool, everything has to be planed with great care and strategy and a variety of healing techniques can be used to achieve almost every possible result. Imagination, intuition and a careful way of thinking is what needed for someone with a bright mind to figure out ways to find multiple uses for a fig wand and its specialty.

Origination: Middle East and Western Asia

Fir (Abies spp.)

Intimidating, Resilient, Solid character.

Fir wood is very resilient and it is great to be used for magick that involves change. Wands made of fir wood are difficult to match, as they will seek the companion of someone who is both resilient, flexible and able to swift and change. All that combined with a very strong character who is solid and avoids to change inside but will adapt and change on the outside.

Fir wands are excellent for transformation spells, techniques and magick that deals with change and shifting. They make fantastic tools for those who practice glamour magick and use enchantments to change the way that someone perceives reality, ideas, feelings etc.

Origination: Asia, Central America, Europe, North Africa

Goncalo Alves (Astronium Fraxinifolium)

Authority, Loyalty.

This is a very rare wood when it comes to the field of wandlore. Wands made of goncalo alves are suited to those who use their abilities and power to maintain authority, in a truthful and non abusive way, because they are loyal to their cause.

Wands made of this wood make some of the best companions for those in the top of hierarchy such as ministers, headmasters etc. as they seek authority and they can be the tool to achieve it. They are also excellent in defensive magick and they can produce powerful charms and magickal seals.

Origination: Brazil

Hawthorn (Crataegus)

Strange and Dual.

Hawthorn is a tree with a strange history associated with healing, as well as with the dark arts. Wands made of hawthorn will seek the companion of someone who is strong, talented and determined, but strangely sometimes they might pair well with someone who is in a very "unbalanced" state, as they can help someone to find their path and amplify their power.

Hawthorn wands are great for both removing and casting powerful curses and healing magick. Healing by the use of a hawthorn wand is very effective, especially for those who have been affected or in a way damaged by a curse. They are also excellent to increase the accuracy of spells and for warding.

Origination: Europe and Northern Asia

Hawthorn

Hazel (Corylus Avellana)

The Healer, The White-one, Sensitivity.

It is the wood of love, freedom, healing and creativity. Wands made of hazel will seek a white companion, someone sensitive who's power is driven by their emotions. Although, it will work best with those who are "driving" their emotions, those who can manage and control their feelings in order to use them in the correct way to power their magickal working.

Hazel wands are all-purpose wands and they are excellent for charms, love spells, beauty spells, glamour and summoning. They also have a unique ability, and this is water detection.

Origination: Europe and Western Asia

Hickory (Carya Floridana)

The Naturalist, The Balanced, The Spiritual.

The hickory wood is an elemental wood. This means that it draws its power from the available elements in their environmental vicinity and that it works wonders when it comes to elemental magick. It is not as common for wandmaking in Europe, due to its nativity.

Hickory wands match well with companions of good intentions who are in touch with nature. They are excellent for charms that create balance and they work amazingly well for those who are exploring spirituality.

Origination: United States of America

Holly (Ilex Aquifolium)

The Protector, Goodness.

Holly is considered to be probably the best wood for protection and defensive magick. Holly wands will seek a companion with inner strength and goodwill. Even though a wand made of holy is the best at defensive magick, it will only work to its true potential with a companion that really needs to be protected and to defend themselves, and not for someone who just feels insecure and wants a layer of extra protection and a sense of security.

Holly wands are ideal for those who seek adventure, challenges and engage in combat in order to protect themselves, their loved ones and to defend and maintain what is fair and right.

Origination: United Kingdom

Hornbeam (Carpinus spp.)

Sentient, Personal, Determined.

Hornbeam is a great wood for wands that are versatile and can become lifetime companions. It is also said that they bring luck to their owners, according to Chinese tradition. Wands made of hornbeam are indifferent to paths, the good or evil. The only path they adapt to is the path of their companion. Hornbeam wand owners are almost always those, passionate about their goals, and those who try to be achievers of their dreams, no matter what their dreams are.

These wands are excellent loyal wands and great for any kind of spell as long as it agrees with their companion's personal morals and wishes.

Origination: North temperate regions and especially Eastern Asia

Ivy (Hedera Helix)

Joy, Fidelity, Protection.

Ivy as a wood is connected with nature, the faerie realm and the ancient Greek god Dionysus. Wands made of ivy will bring joy to their owner and they make very loyal companions.

Ivy wands are great for defensive magick and protection of all sorts, especially when it comes to encounter dark magick. They excel and exceed expectations though when it comes to love and happiness charms.

Origination: Europe and Western Asia

Ivy

Juniper (Juniperus Deppeana)

The Healer.

Juniper is a medical wood, excellent for healing. Wands made of juniper are almost always owned by great healers, although some times they match well with those who need healing too.

They can be used for really demanding healing rituals and spells and they are also very good when it comes to protective magick.

Origination: South United States and Mexico

Lignum Vitae (Guaiacum officinale)

Positivity, Power and Strength.

Lignum Vitae is one of the hardest and most dense woods in the world. The name itself means "Wood of Life" and it is a symbol of the circle of life, of the ending and the beginning of something new. It has been used through the ages for positive magick, especially healing in spiritual and physical matters and energy raising.

Wands made of lignum vitae will find their perfect match in those with a "white" heart, those who are engaged in positive working, and who have the ability to achieve great wisdom. These wands are excellent for charms, enchantments, healing and the arcane arts. They also make great divination tools as they aid in the communication with the divine.

Origination: Europe and South America

Macassar Ebony (Diospyros Ebenum)

The Fighter against the Dark Arts.

This wood is a cousin of Gabon Ebony. Macassar ebony is mostly used for defending against dark magick, based on it's properties.

Wands made of macassar ebony are excellent at dispelling and reversing dark magick, lift curses and protect against most practices of the dark arts. They seek a kind companion, someone who fights against darkness, and can become fearless when it comes to protect the others.

Origination: Southern India

Mahogany (Swietenia Mahogani)

Durability, Protection.

Mahogany wood is known for its use on crafting shields to defend against magick and magickal weapons. It can withstand the most extreme of attacks, even the physical hit of a lightning.

Wands made of mahogany can pair with any kind of companion, as long as they are strong and well balanced. Even though most wands can pair with someone who "needs" their properties and not only those who match them, mahogany wands are extremely rare to do so, they need a strong companion to function at their best.

They are excellent for protection and all sorts of defensive magick and will work well for most types of magick, if it agrees to their master's path.

Origination: South and East USA and the islands around Cuba

Maple (Acer Rubrum)

The Ambitious, The Traveler, The Power of Attraction.

Maple is a favourite wood among the wandmakers. It is very resilient, strong and produces wands of great quality that make life-long devoted companions.

Maple wands are known to suit those who are adventurous, that like to explore and are ambitious achievers. They are great tools for cleansing, healing and summoning spells and charms. These wands, have also a tendency on bringing things together through the power of attraction, and this is something that can happen naturally, unintentionally or something that can be forced by the maple wand owner while using this wood's unique ability during magickal working.

Origination: Canada and North-East USA

Maple

Oak (Quercus sp.)

Endurance, The Guardian.

Oak is a very versatile wood that can be used in many areas of magick with the same rates of success without failing or choosing a specific field on its own.

Oak wands are great match for those who see themselves as guardians of any sort (guardians of others, of ideas, of ethics, of traditions, of knowledge etc.) , people with authority, and activists with power who are meant to be liberators.

These wands are excellent for defensive magick and protection spells and brilliant at placing protective enchantments and long-lasting charms on a target, object, being or over a certain area. They are also very good at power spells and perfect for empowering healing charms (either when they are being cast or pre-existing ones).

Origination: North America, North Europe

Pearwood (Pyrus Sp.)

The Kind Soul, Generosity.

This is a wood of white magick. Wands made of pearwood are excellent for protection against dark magick and most kinds of the dark arts. They are also perfect in magick and techniques that involve or aim at love and joy, and they are some of the most proper tools to cast happiness charms.

They are very resilient and strong, and they can produce very powerful magick, some would say "power ideal for destructive spells". Although it has been noticed that pearwood wands are almost always owned by kind masters with warm hearts, friendly and with cheerful personalities.

Origination: Mediterranean and Asia

Pine (Pinus Ponderosa and Eastern Pines)

Diversity, Longevity, Healing.

Pine wood is a very diverse and versatile wood. Wands made of pine wood are great for healing, protecting and preservation charms. They also work really well for those who practice the art of divination, in general through their lives, as they can form a better spiritual connection between them.

A wand like that, will mostly seek a white companion, with survival skills, that is of good intentions and manners. It has been noticed that pine wood wand owners, tend to have nice, long and prosperous lives.

Finally, these wands are great for cleansing and purification spells and rituals, and some of the best, exquisite wands for non-verbal spellcasting, especially when spiritual and mental connections are formed between the wand and its owner.

Origination: North America and Mediterranea

Purpleheart (Peltogyne)

Psychic Abilities, Wisdom.

Purpleheart wood is a bit uncommon in wandmaking. This wood has been used in divination and spiritual work a lot through the ages and has a great connection to the spirit realm and the aetheric plane.

Purpleheart wands seek the companion of those who are in touch with their inner self, those of a brilliant mind, that possess strong psychic abilities. They are great for protection and defensive magick and excel when it comes to practices that involve psychic powers, spirituality and divination. When psychic-spiritual bonds are created between wand and owner, they make an excellent tool for non-verbal spellcasting.

Origination: Central and South America

Redwood (Sequoia Sempervirens)

Durability, Healing, Spirituality.

This is a wood indifferent to the path that is been followed by its "user", as long as it is been used for healing and spiritual purposes. This mean that it doesn not matter if one wants to use this wood to heal the dark or the light, redwood will always work well and serve its purpose.

A wand made of redwood, will seek the companion of a passionate individual. Someone with the skills of a healer and a high level of spiritual awareness. Such wands are very good for charms that deal with love and emotions in general and they excel when it comes to healing spells and rituals in both physical and spiritual matters.

Origination: The West of the USA

Rosewood (Machaerium Schleroxylon)

The Lover, Spirituality.

Rosewood is a type of wood that can be characterised as a magickally talented wood. Wands made of rosewood need the companion of those who see themselves mostly as spiritual beings, then as emotional and then as physical ones. And those who have the soul of a true lover.

They are great for most kinds of magick and magickal paths but they are excellent tools for divination, healing and love charmwork.

Origination: Central-South America and some parts of Asia

Rowan (Sorbus Aucuparia)

Warmth, The Guardian.

Rowan is known to be the most protective of all woods against all forces of magick, with an extra specialty against faery magick. Wands made of rowan are known to produce the strongest of shield and protective charms, that are extremely hard to break. They seek the companion of those with a warm, kind heart, who have the spirit of a protector and are people of virtue.

Rowan wands are probably the best at protective and defensive magick and they are also excellent at healing charms, warding and divination.

Origination: Central Asia and the British Isles

Silver Lime (Tilia Tomentosa)

Mystery, Unique, Clairvoyance.

This is one of the most exquisite woods across the wandmaking tradition and among the wandmaker circles. It is a very unusual and beautiful wood that makes some of the most elegant of wands.

Wands made of silver lime wood, are excellent for oracles, seers and those who practice various kinds of the art of divination, and especially those who have an elegant spellcasting way. These wands are good almost for any kind of spell and path of magick, but they excel when it comes to arts connected with the divine.

Origination: Europe

Silver Lime

Spruce (Picea)

Versatility, Dominance, Strangeness.

This is one of the strangest woods that are used in the art of wandmaking. This is because spruce wands tend to have such extremely peculiar "personalities" that is difficult to find the proper companion.

Although, they are very versatile wands that are great for almost any kind of spells and form of magick, thus, when they find their ideal partner they can perform the most outstanding of spells.

Origination: The Boreal regions of Earth

Sycamore (Platanus Occidentalis)

Growth, Endurance.

Sycamore is one of the sacred trees that are been used in wandmaking. Wands made of this wood are very versatile and adaptable to any path, magickal technique, casting style and personal preferences. A sycamore wand will seek a companion of lively temper and adventurous nature to find its perfect match.

Wands made of sycamore are excellent for spells of growth, vitality and also strengthening, healing and restoring charms. They are also been used in potionmaking.

Origination: South-East USA

Sycamore

Vine (Vitis Viniferous)

The Visionary, Spirituality.

Another very uncommon, almost rare, wood for wands is vine. It is a very versatile and adaptable wood. Wands made of vine will only work successfully to their true potential in the hands of the right companion. This has to be someone with a brave and surprising personality that has a great purpose to fulfill in their life, a higher goal, or a very meaningful target.

Vine wands are excellent for healing spells, although they will work well for almost any kind of magick if their master really wants to use it or cast it. They are very "peculiar" and some times are collected as curios even by those who don't mean to ever use them in their practice or daily life.

Origination: Europe and Western Asia

Vine

Walnut (Juglans Regia)

Innovation, Intelligence.

Walnut is an extremely versatile and easily adaptable wood that can be used to make excellent wands for those who possess a brilliant mind. Wands made of walnut are indifferent to the path their owners choose, this is because they attract an intelligent companion that will most likely make wise choices of actions, thus there is a trust between wand and master.

Walnut wands are overall great wands for any kind of magick and they can produce any spell their master truly desires. Limitations apply to the skill of their master, the quality of the wood, the core (if there is any) and the circumstances, but not to the abilities of the wood on its own.

Origination: The Region from Balkans to the Himalayas

Wenge (Millettia Laurentii)

Strength and Versatility.

Also known as faux ebony (fake ebony), wenge is a very dark, strong and versatile wood. It is not as commonly used as other woods in wandmaking or magick in general, probably because of its origination, and also of the other most available options which have similar properties.

Wenge wands seek the companion of those who are strong and determined. They are excellent tools to be used against dark magick, as they can cast very strong protective, defensive and dispelling spells. They are also very good in the field of charmwork.

Origination: Congo

Willow (Salix Sepulcralis – Salix Alba)

Diversity, Enchanting.

Willow is a very unusual but not rare wood to be used in wandmaking. It is known for its diversity when it comes to different kinds of practice and paths, and also for its great healing powers.

Wands made of willow will follow anyone who has great ambitions and the potential to achieve their goals and fulfill their dreams and most great desires. These wands are good for weather magick, funerary rites and protection. Although they are excellent when it comes to healing magick of any form, workings that involve psychic abilities and glamour charms.

Origination: Northern Hemisphere, Europe and Western/Central Asia

Willow

Yew (Taxus Baccata)

Death, Dark Magick, Transformation.

Yew is one of the rarest woods in the tradition of wandlore. It is associated with death, reincarnation and the underworld. Wands made of yew are indifferent to their masters' path and they can suit as a perfect companion from the most notorious villain to the greatest hero.

Yew wands are excellent for dark magick, the art of necromancy, transformation and illusion charms including glamour magick, shielding of most sorts and the art of divination. They are also some of the best tools to be used for persuasion charms and casting/placing curses.

Origination: Europe, Asia and Africa

Yew

BIRTH THREES

Many practitioners, especially in the areas around the United Kingdom, choose their wand based on the Celtic Tree Astrology. According to this type of astrology, every person has the sign of a tree based on the date of the day they were born, which is very similar to the idea of zodiac signs. It just comes from a different culture.

This can be proven a tricky choice. It can work in an excellent way for some because it might actually match their personality based on their birthday, but for some others, might be proven very counter effective because date correspondences are not as powerful as a person's true nature. If one wants to pick a wand based on their tree sign, then they must make their full Celtic horoscope and pick carefully as the following chart is simply rough guidelines on trees per date.

> December 24 – January 20:   Birch
> January 21 – February 14:   Rowan
> February 18 – March 17:   Ash
> March 18 – April 14:   Alder
> April 15 – May 12:   Willow
> May 13 – June 9: Hawthorn
> June 10 – July 7:   Oak
> June 8 – August 4:   Holly
> August 5 – September 1:   Hazel
> September 2 – September 29:   Vine
> September 30 – October 27:   Ivy
> October 28 – November 24:   Reed
> November 25 – December 23:   Elder

PHYSICAL PROPERTIES OF WOOD

Of course not only the magickal properties of a wood are been taken into account when crafting a wand. Physical properties are also very important as they will be those to determine the corporeal properties of a wand, its body in the physical world. Also, the physicality of the wood most times, interestingly enough, matches the personality of the wand's owner. These physical properties are the hardness, the rigidity, the elasticity, the strength and the flexibility of the wood.

WOODS BY HARDNESS

A way to classify the woods used in wandmaking is to define their hardness. In the old days, wood hardness was measured by scratching the wood by the use of a cast iron rod pulled down by the force of a ten pound weight. The smaller the scratch the harder the wood was and the greater the scratch the softer the wood. Of course in modern days we have found more sophisticated methods of measuring the hardness. One of them is the use of the Janka hardness test.

During the Janka hardness test, an 11.28mm steel ball is placed on a wood piece , which is a sample of the chosen wood to be tested, and then a weight is applied on it. The desirable result is for the ball to be inserted in the wood by half it's diameter. The weight/force required for the ball to be embedded in it is then measured in pounds-force also marked as lbf.

The higher the number in the Janka scale the harder the wood.

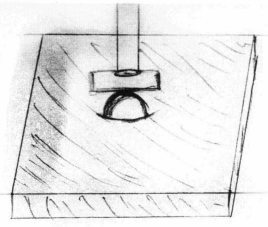

Janka scale in pounds-force (lbf) from Hardest to Softest.

Lignum Vitae:	4.500
Ebony:	3.220
Bloodwood:	2.900
Pearwood:	2.732
Purpleheart:	2.713
Bocote:	2.200
Goncalo Alves:	2.160
Dogwood:	2.150
Canarywood:	2.000
Hickory:	1.820
Rosewood:	1.780
Hornbeam:	1.780
Applewood:	1.730
Australian Blackwood:	1.720
Wenge:	1.630
Yew:	1.600
Black Laurel:	1.510
Maple:	1.500
Cypress:	1.375
Oak:	1.360
Ash:	1.320
Beech:	1.300
Walnut:	1.290
Birch:	1.260
Elm:	1.200
Juniper:	1.160
Cocobolo:	1.136
Eucalyptus:	1.125
Avodire:	1.080
Black Walnut:	1.010
Maple (soft):	950
Cherry:	950
Cedar:	900

Elder:	840
Mahogany:	800
Sycamore:	770
Alder:	590
Willow:	568
Chestnut:	540
Black Limba:	490
Redwood:	480
Spruce:	480
Pine:	460
Aspen:	420
Fir:	407
Buckeye:	350

WOODS BY RIGIDITY - ELASTICITY

The rigidity and the elasticity is something that cannot be easily determined in every wood. Varies to the quality of the wood, the amount/percentage of humidity in it and many other aspects. Do not confuse though the ability of a wood to bend with flexibility. A flexible wood is the one that can bend easily and also be strong enough not to break while maintaining it's original shape.

When it comes to wands, the woods used are each with it's own qualities, percentage of humidity etc. and these aspects vary from the industrial wood which has a certain percentage of humidity, is chemically treated etc. In wand making the wood bending is measure in a scale from 1 to 21 where 1 is the easiest to bend and 21 the hardest.

The wood denting scale has as follows.

Juniper:	4,48
Cedar:	6,07
Willow:	7,20
Pearwood:	7,80
Buckeye:	8,07
Redwood:	8,41
Chestnut:	8,48
Applewood:	8,76
Pine:	8,90
Mahogany:	9,31
Yew:	9,31
Alder:	9,52
Sycamore:	9,79
Aspen:	9,86
Cypress:	9,93
Spruce:	10,20
Fir:	10,24

Elm:	10,25
Cherry:	10,30
Black Limba:	10,49
Walnut:	10,81
Birch:	10,97
Avodire:	11,13
Maple:	11,31
Black Walnut:	11,59
Hornbeam:	11,68
Hickory:	11,72
Oak:	11,81
Beech:	11,86
Ash:	12,00
Bocote:	12,19
Black Laurel:	12,46
Dogwood:	13,26
Rosewood:	13,50
Australian Blackwood:	14,82
Canarywood:	14,93
Goncalo Alves:	16,56
Ebony:	16,89
Wenge:	17,59
Cocobolo:	18,70
Purpleheart:	20,26
Bloodwood:	20,78

Some times the characteristic rigidity of the wood of someone's wand can say a lot about its owner's personality. There is a vast variety of such characteristics, such as : stiff, flexible, pliable, supple, unyielding, brittle, springy, resilient etc.

WOODS BY STRENGTH

The Modulus of Rupture, also abbreviated as MOR, is a scale that measures the strength of a wood before its breaking point. This measures the overall, ultimate strength of a wood to it's breaking point, overcoming all aspects of rigidity, elasticity, and hardness.

It is measures by pound-force per square inch (lbf/in^2).

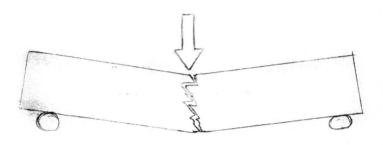

The scale of Strength, by the modulus of rapture from the strongest to the weakest wood has as follows.

Bloodwood:	25.290
Ebony:	22.930
Cocobolo:	22.910
Purpleheart:	22.000
Wenge:	21.990
Hickory:	20.200
Canarywood:	19.080
Applewood:	18.650
Rosewood:	16.970
Dogwood:	16.720
Bocote:	16.590
Eucalyptus:	16.200
Birch:	15.570

Avodire:	15.400
Mahogany:	15.260
Yew:	15.200
Australian Blackwood:	15.020
Ash:	15.000
Beech:	14.900
Black Walnut:	14.650
Oak:	14.460
Maple:	13.030
Black Laurel:	12.740
Black Limba:	12.510
Cherry:	12.360
Walnut:	12.250
Elm:	12.080
Pearwood:	12.080
Cypress:	11.400
Sycamore:	10.000
Alder:	9.800
Fir:	9.580
Pine:	9.500
Spruce:	9.450
Chestnut:	9.340
Redwood:	8.950
Juniper:	8.940
Cedar:	8.800
Aspen:	8.400
Willow:	8.150
Buckeye:	7.500

WOODS AND FLEXIBILITY

As it is already mentioned, the elastic qualities, the precise flexibility of each wood are hard to be determined because of a large number of factors. Although there are some wand quality woods that have almost always the same "rigidity" qualities. They are separated in the following five categories.

Very Flexible:
Blackthorn
Dogwood
Elm
Hawthorn
Hickory
Hornbeam
Lignum Vitae
Oak
Purpleheart

Quiet Springy:
Ash
Beech
Goncalo Alves
Juniper
Pearwood

Fairly Stiff & Solid:
African Blackwood
Birch
Bloodwood
Cherry
Cocobolo
Ebony (it is also pliable within reason)
Macassar Ebony

Walnut
Wenge

Slightly Unbending:
Alder
Avodire
Chestnut
Fir

Quiet Brittle:
Aspen
Buckeye
Cedar
Pine
Spruce

WANDS AND THEIR MASTER'S PERSONALITY

Most of the times, wands can reflect their masters' personalities. Unless a wand is chosen incorrectly or being inherited, then it can describe its owner's personality to a high accuracy, especially when they are perfectly matched with their companion. Wands and their masters can finely reflect each other's personalities, habits and behaviour.

The majority of wands have special characteristics, for example, some are good for healers, others are good for indifferent practitioners while some others are perfect for those who wish to bring havoc. But that just describes the type of magick that suits best on each wand, and not their masters' personalities. These should not be confused as being the same thing. Someone who is a healer, can have a hard, dark personality who wants only to heal those who are harmful, while someone who is good with the dark arts, might have a soft, bendy heart and possess a very flexible character.

The personality lies mostly on the physical properties of the wand's wood, such as its rigidity, hardness, even length and shape. Here are some examples of how personality can be interpreted and determined by the physical characteristics of each wand.

Alder:
It is a moderately light weight wood but has an intermediate to good strength. This means that it suits better someone with a light heart but intense personality, a wandered who takes risks.

Ash:

It is a heavy strong and stiff wood that it is hard to carve and also has a good shock resistance. So it will match best with someone who possess a very strong character, unbending to their opinions and sometimes a bit stubborn.

Aspen:

Aspen is a lightweight wood, it is soft but is moderately stiff. Its low shock resistance makes it into a brittle wand. Aspen's master will probably be someone with a pure light heart and fragile feelings but with a stiff and strong character, a very dual person.

Avodire:

It's a moderately heavy, moderately strong but with a moderately low shock resistance wood. It suits best those who have a strong and intense personality, but will try to avoid conflict.

Beech:

Heavy, strong and hard, but bendy and with high shock resistance. This wood makes an excellent wand for those who are very strong in character but with a very acceptable and tolerant personality.

Birch:

It is a quiet heavy, strong and hard wood with a good shock resistance. Ideal for those who's positive way of thinking gives them strength. Those who can handle any conflict if needed, but will avoid conflict as a first option.

Black Walnut:

It is a heavy, hard, strong and stiff wand but also has a great shock resistance. All these, make it a wood excellent for the wands of those who possess a very strong character, that stand by their opinions and have an unbending personality.

Buckeye:

It is a very light and weak wood, very soft and of low shock resistance. This wood makes brittle wands which means that a buckeye wand owner will be someone with a very quiet personality, probably shy, who will try to avoid conflict at all costs.

Cedar:

Cedar is a lightweight wood, not too strong, a bit soft and with low shock resistance. It has though very low stiffness index, which makes it "brittle" yet flexible. Suits best someone with a kind heart, a quiet, sensitive and resilient individual that is ready to swift to a fighter when needed.

Cherry:

It is a strong, stiff and a bit hard wood. Makes an ideal match with someone who stands strong, and possess an unbending personality, without being too hard to others. Someone strange and well balanced.

Chestnut:

Chestnut is a light weight wood, moderately hard, with an average/low strength and a low shock resistance. It is best for someone with a soft heart, nourishing and kind. Someone who can stand to protect the ones they love even though s/he knows that they might not make it. It has the soft, nourishing and protective personality of a mother.

Ebony:

It is one of the hardest woods in the world, very dense, strong, solid, with a moderate shock resistance, average flexibility and it is also one of the most expensive woods. Its ideal companion is someone with a very strong character, solid mind and unyielding personality. A person who is able to withstand a lot of pressure and challenges and is powerful enough to deal with any obstacle. Most of the times those who match with ebony are imaginative, excited but yet dominant with an expensive luxurious taste.

Due to its strength and resilience, some think that they can keep bending and forcing strength and pressure to that wood indefinitely. That is until it suddenly snaps and creates hard sharp splinters. That reflects perfectly the personality of their companion when they are perfectly matched.

~Advice~ Never push too hard or test an ebony wand's owner's patience for an extended period of time. When cross their limits, they tend to burst in the most unpredictable ways and during the least expected time. This can be proven dangerous and most of the times it comes in an emotionally cold and event violent way.

Elm:

Elm is a very hard wood but it is also very bendy, flexible with a high shock resistance. It is ideal for those who are neutral, indifferent and strong. Most times elm finds the ideal companion to someone very sophisticated and with elegant ways.

Fir:

A lightweight wood, soft, medium strength with a low shock resistance, but it is somehow pliant. Which means it suits someone with a stiff character who is intimidating in order to protect their fragile hidden personality. But someone who is also very resilient when needed as well.

Goncalo Alves:

This is a very durable, very strong and yet very flexible wood. It suits best those with a very strong character, authoritative personality and the ability to manage almost anything that comes their way. Those who are loyal to their cause and ideas and seek to maintain order. It is also an excellent indicator of someone who doesn't give up.

Hickory:

Hickory is a heavy, hard and strong wood. Its ideal matching personality will be a strong and steady individual with a balanced inner self.

Mahogany:

This is a strong dense wood with an average/good durability. Suits best those who prefer to keep a rather passive attitude. Those who will prefer to find pure defensive ways in the means of durability to protect themselves, instead of using offensive ones.

Oak:

Oak is a very heavy, strong and very durable wood. Its ideal companion is someone with an extremely strong and resilient personality. Usually someone with an intimidating nature and an inner wisdom, destined to become a guardian or mentor.

Pine:

It is a lightweight, soft and of low strength wood. It has low shock resistance but a low stiffness index which make it fairly pliable. Ideal for those who will try to avoid conflict, have a soft personality and are quiet in general. Pine companions tend to live long, because even at the hardest of periods they are finding ways to avoid danger, heal what is damaged and navigate through obstacles.

Purpleheart:

This is a very strong, hard and heavy, one of the most unbending woods. It matches best to someone with extremely strong, stable and unyielding personality, who can withstand a lot and can survive through extreme situations. It is colour indicates someone with exceptional psychic abilities too.

Redwood:

This is a light-weighed wood, but moderately strong, stiff and quiet hard. Suits best someone indifferent, adaptable and easy to shift from quiet, soft and weak to loud, strong and durable.

Rosewood:

Hard, heavy and very durable, rosewood finds its best match among those who are very stable, and passionate. Rosewood wands are found to belong mostly to those who have a taste of luxury and have an elegant and yet solid way of spellcasting.

Spruce:

It is a very versatile wood. Not too heavy not too light, neither hard or soft, resistant to shock or not... With an average stiffness and bending ability. Spruce wands mostly match with those who are very versatile, diverse and easy to shift according to the needs and current circumstances. Their companion tends to be rather strange and bipolar.

Sycamore:

Sycamore is a moderately heave wood, with moderate hardness, stiffness and a good shock resistance. Its perfect match is someone very versatile and resilient who can withstand a lot. Someone who is easily adaptable to most situations and who has a strong personality.

MAGICK CORES

MAGICK CORES

Depending on the tradition and the wandmaker, magick wands contain magickal cores or are infused with magickal essences. Some of them can have both, but this might make the wand's use very specific and too complex.

The cores and essences enhance the wood's attributes and give the wand its magical abilities.

The core:

Is found deep inside the wand, either in a cavity in the wand's handle or in the middle of it across the full length of the wand. It can be made of different materials such as crystals, magick conductors, organic matter from different beings etc.

The essence:

Is embedded in the entire wood. It works in the form of a liquid that keeps the essence in it, and then is the wood that soaks in the solution for a period of time to become imbued with it. The essence can be made of various ingredient, can be a potion, a body fluid, the essence of a creature trapped in a liquid etc.

Essences won't be covered or listed in this book as they are custom, vary and do not fall under common or uncommon categories. Even when the same type of liquid essence is used, each wandmaker tends to use their own variation which makes it impossible to categorise with precision.

CLASSIFICATION OF CORES

The most known cores are separated into five different categories. The common, the uncommon, the unusual, the rare and the supreme.

Common Cores:

Are the cores that have been most commonly used by the wand makers. They are also easy to find and most "abundant" as materials compared to the rest of the core categories. All the above make them more affordable and this is another reason why they are so commonly used. They are also most common because of their high success rate as "materials" to work correctly with almost every wand without being too specialised.

Uncommon Cores:

Are the cores that are a bit harder to find, and are used less in wand making than the common cores. They can be used though with the same success as with every other core listed here.

Unusual Cores:

Are the cores that have either strange properties or that are unusual to find in a wand, not only because of their rarity but also because they are made of things that make an unusual choice for a core. They tend to be strange options and create very unique combinations when they match with the wood for a wand.

Rare Cores:

Cores in this category are named rare, solely because they are made of components that are very difficult to find. Also because they might be extremely expensive to afford in comparison with other cores. In any case they are cores that are actually rare to find in wands no matter what the reason.

Supreme Cores:

These cores are the ones that have been characterised by the most reputable wandmakers as the best qualified substances to make excellent magickal cores, capable to produce the most powerful and accurate magick.

Multi-Cores:

This is a special category of cores that can apply to all of the above five categories as it has little to nothing to do with the rarity of them. They are cores made of different ingredients, such as powders, body parts, plants, minerals, alloys etc. Such as Electrum Magicum and other cores of power.

Multi-cores have to be selected very carefully and be custom made for each wand owner by a very skilful core maker or a master potion maker.

EXAMPLES OF CORES

These are only examples of the most known non-custom/personalised cores. Personalised cores are not possible to be listed, as they are far too many, actually an unknown number and most of the makers keep their components secret.

COMMON CORES

Amethyst
This is a quiet common core with great qualities for healing and protection spells, for spells that have to do with breaking or lifting illusions. It is best for this core to exist in the wand of someone who is using psychic powers and clairvoyance.

Black Cat's Hair
An excellent core for any kind of magick and for anything relevant to the mysteries of the occult and the world. It does not have a specialty, it helps the same with every spell or path and practice.

Copper – Cuprum Metallicum
It is one of the most common materials that is been used in wand making, for cores, inlays and more. Some even make whole wands completely out of copper.

It is not classified as a supreme core though, despite its power, it is not very versatile as the supreme cores are, as it has an "incline" towards white magick and love spells.

It is a fantastic core when it comes to spells about love, beauty, relationships, balance and artwork. Also aids significantly in healing rituals.

Fox's Hair

An excellent core for those who specialise in spells/charms of transformation and illusions. Those who are exceptionally smart, agile, with fast reactions and who prefer action over theory.

Owl's Feather

This is one of the most versatile cores, great for any kind of magick. It helps the master of the wand that lies in to increase their intuition ability and to achieve true wisdom.

Peacock's Feather

A very common core, although its abilities are a bit more specified. Like every other core, it will produce all sorts of magick but is specialises in spells about beauty, glamour and rebirth, and will help its companion to achieve wisdom of the mystic arts.

Quartz – Silicon Dioxide

It is considered one of the most magickal minerals/substances of the physical world. Its exceptional ability to adapt and its versatility, along with its unique ability to be "programmed" for any purpose , make quartz crystal one of the most useful, reputable and desired cores. It is also known that quartz not only channels, but also amplifies the user's magickal energy.

UNCOMMON CORES

Moss Agate

It is one of the most uncommon cores. Moss agate provides great control and power for spells over healing and every spell of astral nature. It has been noticed that masters of wands with a moss agate core also possess great psychic and natural healing powers.

Onyx

This is an excellent core for those who want to excel in protective and defensive magick. Its qualities make it brilliant for protection against dark magick and for dispelling it. It is also great for spells of transformation and charmwork.

Onyx aids the master of the wand that it lies in to achieve balance and to get spiritual inspiration.

Raven's Feather

It's a fantastic core for any kind of magick. It does not have a certain specialty, therefore it is great for all sorts of spellcasting and all mysteries involved with the mundane, the magickal world and the arcane knowledge. Raven's feather aids to absorbing and using power and helps especially to draw power from the subconscious.

Raven's Feather

Silver – Argentum Nitricum

An exceptionally powerful core, always associated with magick. Promotes psychic abilities and balance and its power is guided by its master's emotion. Excellent for any kind of spell, especially protective ones and for handling/dispelling negative energy and dark magick.

Wolf's Hair

Wolf's hair is known as the core best to be used for totem magick, protection spells and defensive charms. It also promotes its master's spirituality.

UNUSUAL CORES

Bear's Fur

This is a core that helps to draw power from the subconscious. It grants great strength to the master of the wand that lies in and it is one of the best cores to be used for protection charms and defensive magick. Its masters tend to be practitioners with nourishing and caring personalities.

Haematite

Haematite is a core with some sort of specific qualities. Even though it can be used to produce most sorts of spells, it is best used for protection, and to maintain authority by those who will achieve a rank in authority and have the soul of a warrior.

Magnet

It is one of the best cores when it comes to energy handling. Magnets are great for any kind of spell and every magickal path. Although, they can show their true power when it comes to the use of binding spells and charmwork.

Tiger's Eye

This is a core capable to produce extremely powerful protection. Its magic is driven by its masters emotions so the protective properties are awakened by instinct. It promotes its masters strong will and courage. It is also very good for charms that are relevant with bravery.

RARE CORES

Amber

Amber creates magnetism and perfect charge for spells. It has a strong power for both white and dark magick and suits best those who are indifferent to paths by their nature. It empowers all sorts of spells and excels at charms about protection and attraction spells.

Electrum Magicum

This is one of the rarest among the cores and one of the most famous multi-cores. It is also very pricey and very difficult to create. Electrum Magicum is an alchemical substance made of :

> 3 parts iron
> 5 parts lead
> 6 parts tin
> 15 parts copper
> 15 parts mercury
> 30 parts silver
> and 30 parts gold

Probably one of the most powerful cores if made correctly. Its making process is known only to the most skilled core makers and alchemists, it is also a dangerous process as it can cause poisoning and mental disfunction because of the lead and mercury. It can produce the strongest, finest of magick for any kind of spell.

Gold – Aurum Metallicum

This is the core of vitality. A very powerful substance that promotes creativity. It seeks to be used by those in authority and gives power for any kind of spell and any sort of magick. It is rare both because of its price and also because it is not usual to find it even among the wealthy practitioners.

Lion's Hair

Cores made of Lion's hair (always the mane of a male lion) are only found in the wands of those with extreme power and great hearts. Lion's hair promote bravery and they are best used by those with authority and great leadership skills and potentials.

Platinum

It is one of the most multidimensional substances. Cores made of platinum are among the best to be used to transfer magick between worlds and to cast spells from one realm to another.

Platinum can be used for any kind of magick, even though it "hates" to be used for mundane daily tasks. It promotes sight and helps to achieve wisdom and to find one's true path.

Ruby

This core represents life, life's power and vitality. It gives great strength and promotes courage. It can be used to amplify one's powers and almost any kind of spell. Ruby works best for spells to maintain and preserve life and protection charms, but not as well for spells who cause death and are of a decreasing nature.

SUPREME CORES

Black Cat's Hair
Electrum Magicum
Owl's Feather
Quartz Crystal
Raven's Feather

NOTE: Non flexible cores such as minerals are not suitable for long cores across the wand's length, as they are not pliable, they will shatter when the wand bends or faces a shock.

WAND'S LENGTH

Wands come in various lengths (most of them in the range between ten and fifteen inches) and there is an association between the length of the wand and the build of the practitioner's body and their personality.

For example, regarding the physical body, long wands tend to belong to tall owners, where short ones tend to be owned by shorter practitioners. A six feet seven inches tall practitioner, is very common to have a sixteen inches long wand, where a five feet five inches tall one, it is very common to have a twelve inches long wand.

On the other hand it is not rare to see a five feet ten inches tall practitioner, having a fifteen inches long wand, because this has also to do with their personality and the way they cast spells.

Besides the height now, long wands tend to suit practitioners with big personalities and those with a commodious, voluminous and dramatic style of spellcasting and magickal practice. Short wands on the other hand, tend to suit those with "quiet" personalities, maybe even personalities that lack of something or those with a more of a narrow and incommodious, kind of cramped style of casting magick.

WAND'S SHAPE

Same as length, wands come in a variety of shapes too. Neat wands tend to be attracted by those with a refined, precise and elegant way of spell-casting, when irregular, crooked and stubbly wands tend to be attracted by those with a crude, heedless or inadvertent way of spell-casting.

TECHNICAL ADVICE

Wands can be crafted by either the use of a wood lathe machine (electric powered or hand turned) or be hand carved with various tools. For the wood lathe machine, the heart of the tree or thick wide unprocessed branches can be used. Not the milled, treated wood planks and beams that someone can find in a timber yard. For hand carving, branches is the best option to be used, for their unique shape, as carving gives a freedom of form and shape.

Treated wood should be avoided as most of them are not simply cut, but are treated with chemicals which alter the consistency and natural properties of each wood, and make it no longer be of wand quality. Use only natural wood. The wood can be used with or without its bark, but should always be turned or carved once it's dry. Remove the bark from the parts you don't want it to be, before you dry the wood.

WOOD LATHE WANDS

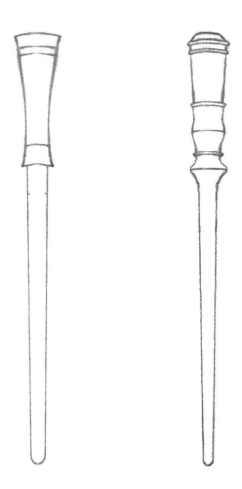

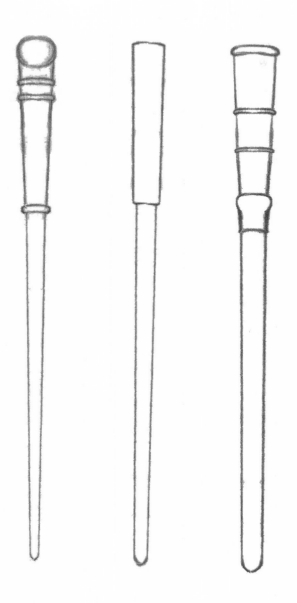

HAND CARVED WANDS

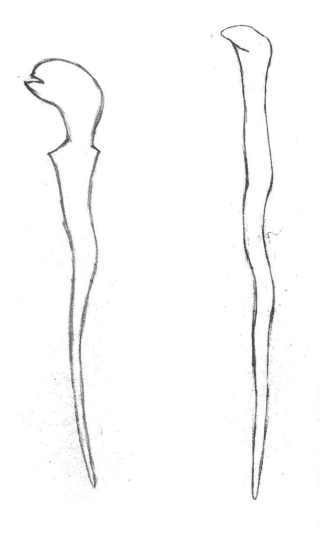

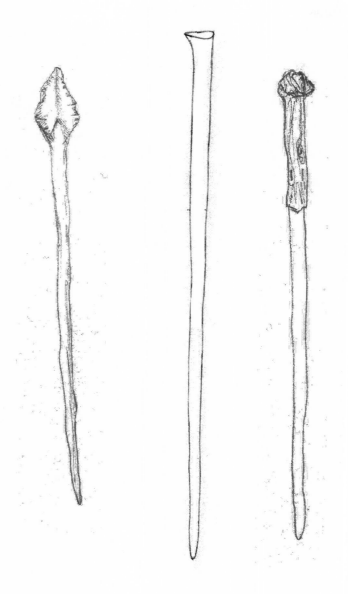

PARTS OF THE WAND

Almost all wands are made to have the two basic parts. The handle and the shaft. The handle is most times shorter and it's the part that one holds the wand from. It can be decorated with an extension of a crystal/stone, wood or metal. The shaft is the elongated part of the wand and some time it can have an extension made of crystal/stone too.

Although, some wands might be divided in more parts based on their design and some others might have only one single part and they look as a straight stick without a defined division point between handle and shaft.

- One needs to pay great attention especially on the crafting of the handle. It has to have the right texture and feel on it and also have a nice grip so it feels practical to use and handle. That combined with all the decoration and other aesthetics of the wand should be taken into account when designing it. Its appearance should not stand as an obstacle to its practical way of use.

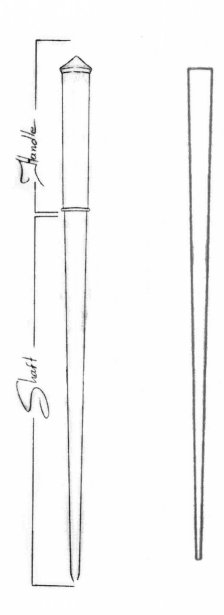

EXAMPLES OF HANDLES

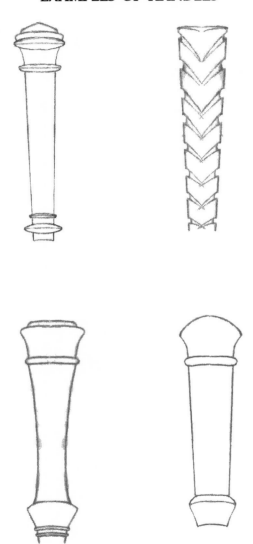

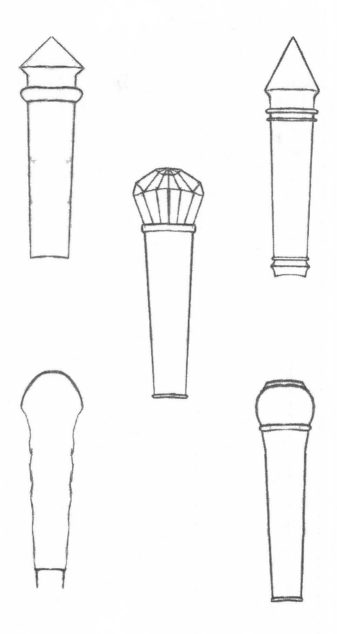

THE CORE

To insert a core, the wand has to be drilled once it is finished.

For a handle core, drill the back of the handle and through it, to create enough space for the core. Insert the core material and then close the hole with wood from the same piece of wood that the wand is made of.

File or trim the excess wood and polish. It can be just an insertion of a splinter of cork shaped piece, it can even be an ornamental piece of wood to finish the handle.

For a core across the length of the wand, drill a very fine hole, from end to end of the full length of the wand, insert the core and finish the same way as with the handle core. If the long core is soft or for any other reason need to be inserted with a needle, then drill across the length of the wand till both ends are completely open for a needle to pass through and then seal and finish them both with the above way.

NOTE: All cores are able to produce any kind of magick at some level, same as wands, they have just certain characteristics to add to and specialisations.

TOOLS

There are many tools that can be used in wandmaking. Almost anything can be used as a tool and each wandmaker has invented their own custom tools through the years. For every wandmaker though, there are some basic, fundamental tools that they use and these are the same tools that almost every single apprentice wandmaker starts with.

Carving Blades

The carving blades come in many shapes and sizes. The most common are the straight carving knife, which is a very sharp straight blade used for any kind of carving. Very skilled wandmakers can create complete wands just by using this tool.

The curved carving knife, is a blade which comes in a bended form and it's used mostly to peel off bark or parts of the wood.

The V-blade, is a straight blade with a v shaped edge, used to carve very detailed features and streams in the wood. This is mostly used around the handle of each wand.

Saw

Saws come in various sizes. They have very sharp teeth, used to cut through wood. From thin branches to whole trees. Very small saws can also be used to carve decorative rings and lines on the wands.

Rasps and Files

These tools are used for shaping. They grate the wood with their surfaces which are coated with a large amount of metallic small teeth. Some are very coarse while some are very fine. They come in many shapes and sizes, the most popular are the flat, the triangular, the curved and the round one.

Drill

A hand powered fine drill, is proven to be the most appropriate tool to use while carving the cavity for the core of each wand.

Chisels

These are the best tools to use with a wood lathe machine. They have a great variety of tips that can be used to create almost any possible shape while turning the wood.

Sandpaper

Similar to rasps and files, sandpaper is a more gentle way to remove small amounts of wood. The coarse sand paper can be used for shaping the wand. There is also a very fine sandpaper which is perfect for finishing the wand and makes excellent preparation for the polish to be applied.

The Vise

A padded vise is a great addition to a wandmaker's toolbox. It can firmly hold the wood without someone risking to carve their own hands. The padded grip also protects the wood from being squeezed, scratched or marked in any way.

CARVING TECHNIQUES

There are numerous different techniques for both wood lathe and hand carving. I would not like to influence anyone towards a certain technique or those that I have used, so I will avoid mentioning a certain style. That applies to the decorating and material preferences.

Each wandmaker should be guided by instinct to choose a suitable technique or invent one. If one is lucky enough to start as someone's apprentice, their mentor can guide them and show them samples of different techniques.

A very helpful tip though, no matter which technique one uses, is to mark the wood with a pencil, to have rough guidelines of where and how to carve, in order to minimise mistakes and eliminate possible "damages" in the design.

DECORATIOINS

There are many different things and techniques that wands can be decorated with. The most common are: shapes, inscriptions and letters, sigils and symbols, inlay, stones and crystals, totems, statued and forms.

SHAPES

A wand can be decorated just by carving shapes on it. Wider or narrow parts, swifter sections, bumps and more, can be used to personalise a wand.

SHAPES OF WANDS

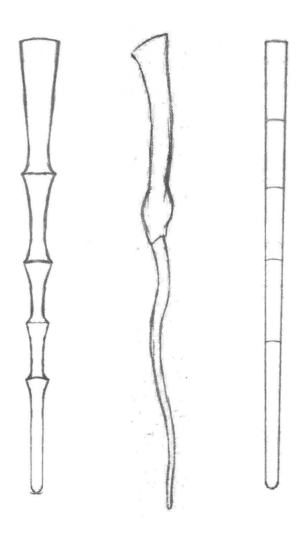

INSCRIPTIONS AND LETTERS

One can decorate a wand by carving simple letters, words of power and even whole inscriptions on it. These not only add to the aesthetics of the wand, but based on what the inscription is, special attributes can be added to it.

SIGILS AND SYMBOLS

Likewise inscriptions and letters, symbols can be added to a wand to give it both aesthetic and magickal attributes.

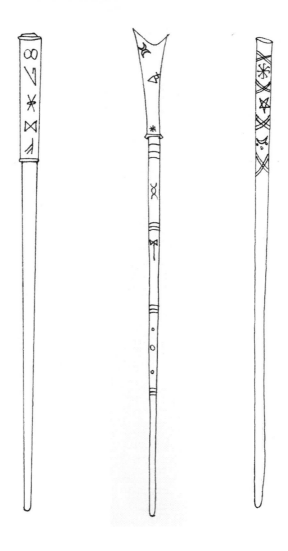

INLAY

This is a technique that can be used to ass shapes, inscriptions, symbols and more to a wand. It works by carving pieces of wood to the desired design and removing small amounts of wood from the design. Then the empty space is filled with other materials. The materials that can be used include woods, crystals and metals (according to their special attributes) that are carved to the appropriate design to fill the cavities.

STONES AND CRYSTALS

They are very popular decorations for wands and they also have practical benefits. Based on the properties of each stone and crystal, the wand can gain additional attributes.

Most wandmakers use stones and crystals for the edge of the handle or the tip of the wand, or both. Although there are some rare wands that almost the entire shaft is made of crystal.

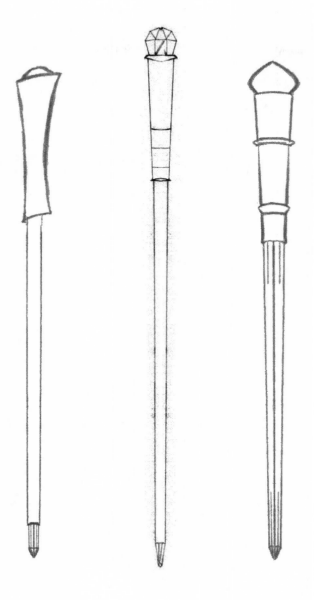

TOTEMS STATUES AND FORMS

Wandmakers who are very skilled with detailed wood carving, often create sculptures on the wand. Either on a certain part of it or even the whole handle can be a totem. Most common is to see a carved form at the edge of the handle.

STAINS AND PAINTING

Some wandmakers use stains to colour the wand or create real art on it by painting it.

I strongly advise against such techniques, as they alter both the physical and magickal properties of the wood, and they might make a wand completely useless for other than decorating purposes. The only "acceptable" method is to use natural aging solutions made of natural ingredients to slightly stain the wood by darkening it to its natural tones.

Caution: Make sure that these ingredients are not opposite to the wand's nature.

FINISHING AND POLISHING

The only acceptable types of finishing for a wand, are either mixes of natural was or natural varnishing oils. Each has to be of the same nature as the wand to be applied safely.

ACTIVATION

ACTIVATION OF THE WAND

After a wand is completed, there are numerous rituals, techniques and spells used to activate it. All master wandmakers create their own activation forms, because this is as custom as the creation of the wand itself.

The wand should not be matched with the identity of the wandmaker, but it has to have its own identity and personality in order to match with its future companion, its owner and master. Most rituals have the same main components and they aim to neutralise the identity and influence of a wand so it can have its "own personality" and be ready to be used by its master and in time to be adapted in their personal style of magick style and path.

Ideas to create a Wand Activation Ritual

- Candles, herbs and incenses of the appropriate properties can be used to charge the wand with neutral power or specific qualities to match its nature.
- Some wandmakers prefer to simply awaken the wand's and the core's inner power as they believe this to be the most accurate way of activating a wand's true power without any personal intentions getting in the way.
- Oils or wax to anoint the wand for the ritual. So finishing and polishing the wand can become part of the activation ritual.
- Write an incantation/spell in which the activation of the wand is stated. Important parts to mention in the incantation/spell are:
  - The power of the wand and core to be awakened.
  - The true qualities of it to show.
  - For it to be released by any attachment and identity until it finds its owner and true master to be matched with.
  - And to have its own sort of consciousness.
- Most wandmakers already have their own wands, so they use them for casting custom activation spells to the wands they make.
  - An activation ritual can be used to create a spell which will be used in the future as a replacement of the ritual directly to the newly made wand to activate it.

Wands can also be part of the standard ritual.

ACTIVATION WITH THE AID OF MAGNETIC FIELDS

The geomagnetic lines can be a very useful and powerful tool to use while activating a wand. Magnetic fields can be used to activate the energy flow in a material or unclog blocked energy when something has already been activated.

Basic understanding of magnets and their field.

The flow in each magnet moves from + to – where + has been named North and – Has been named South. This happens on the outside of the magnet, on the inside the flow moves as in a circuit from the – to + in order to create a continuous flowing movement and allow the flow to continue.

When two or more magnets are been placed together, they form what we call a current, which is the flow of the newly formed magnetic fields and its direction varies based on the positions and placement of the magnets.

Earth's magnetic field now works as an enormous magnet. Although it has been named incorrectly and when we are referring to Earth, + is the South and – is the North, which is the reason that when we use the magnetic needle of a compass, the North+ of the needle shows the North pole of the Earth.

The magnetic flow of earth moves from the South pole to the North pole, but only the names change as the field always moves from the + to the - , therefore on the inside it flows from the North to the South.

North Pole -

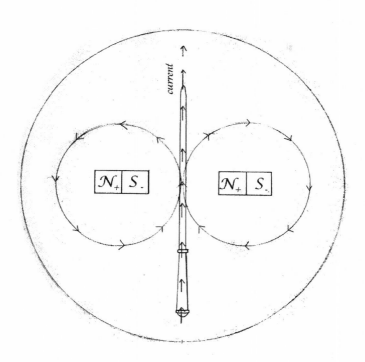

South Pole +

Placement of the Wand

To take advantage of the magnetic fields, one should place the wand correctly during the activation ritual. With the use of a compass, locate the North pole of the earth and place an elongated object such as a pencil, with its bottom showing the South and its tip showing the North so you wont need to do the process again.

Facing the North, place two strong magnets according to the diagram, one on the left with its + on the left and – on the right, leave some space between them so they will not been attracted together and then place a second one in the same manner.

This will create a current from the South pole to the North pole. To activate the flow on the wand we need both the current from the magnets and the current from the earth to pass from the internal structure of the wand. The outer flow of the earth goes from the South pole to the North pole, therefore the wand must be placed between the two magnets and with its tip facing the North pole of the earth, same direction as the pencil. (without the pencil anywhere in the placement)

That creates the perfect placement for the used of the magnetic fields and currents to activate the flow in a wand or to repair a wand that seems to be clogged.

Notes

The crafting of a wand can be very personal or very professional. No matter if one is making a wand for a client or for personal use there should always be a plan for it, to ensure the best possible results and to avoid mistakes. A simple step by step wand crafting guide has as follows:

- Study the wandlore. Do not start crafting a wand without having a good understanding of the art of wandlore.
- Select the proper materials. The wood that will be used for the wand, what its core will be, the decorations etc.
- Design the wand. A simple design on paper if it is for personal use or a very accurate technical design if it is for a client or for a custom order from a wandmaker.
- Carve the wood and decorate so the physical body of the wand is ready for the process.
- Insert the core. With any of the know techniques.
- Finish the decoration of the wand.
- Finish and polish the wand.
- Activate it.

The Author and Publisher take no responsibility on how
the contents of this book will be used by the reader and
what outcome the misuse of these information might have.

WANDLORE

A GUIDE FOR THE APPRENTICE WANDMAKER

K. P. THEODORE

Made in the USA
Middletown, DE
15 October 2020